FRANNY'S WAY

Richard Nelson

BROADWAY PLAY PUBLISHING INC
New York
www.broadwayplaypublishing.com
info@broadwayplaypublishing.com

First printing: September 2003
I S B N: 978-0-88145-216-7

Book design: Marie Donovan
Word processing: Microsoft Word for Windows
Typographic controls: Xerox Ventura Publisher 2.0 P E
Typeface: Palatino
Copy editing: Sue Gilad
Printed on recycled acid-free paper and bound in the U S A

FRANNY'S WAY was first produced by Playwrights
Horizons (Tim Sanford, Artistic Director; Leslie Marcus,
Managing Director; William Russo, General Manager)
on 6 March 2002. The cast and creative contributors
were:

OLDER FRANNY/GRANDMA .... Kathleen Widdoes
YOUNG FRANNY .... Elisabeth Moss
DOLLY .... Domenica Cameron-Scorsese
SALLY ....Yvonne Woods
PHIL .... Jesse Pennington

Director ....Richard Nelson
Set design .... Thomas Lynch
Costume design .... Susan Hilferty & Linda Ross
Lighting design ....Jennifer Tipton
Sound design ....Scott Lehrer
Stage management ....Jane Pole, Kevin Bertolacci
Clare Gardner

FRANNY'S WAY was subsequently produced by
The Geffen Playhouse (Gilbert Cates, Producing
Director; Randall Arney, Artisitic Director; Stephen
Eich, Managing Director) opening on 28 June 2003.
The cast and creative contributors were:

OLDER FRANNY/GRANDMA .... Penny Fuller
YOUNG FRANNY .... Elisabeth Moss
DOLLY .... Domenica Cameron-Scorsese
SALLY .... Susan May Pratt
PHIL ....Jesse Pennington

Director ....Richard Nelson
Set design ....Thomas Lynch
Costume design ....Susan Hilferty
Lighting design .... David Weiner
Sound design .... Scott Lehrer
Stage management ...Elsbeth M Collins, Andrea Iovino

CHARACTERS & SETTING

FRANNY, *seventeen*
DOLLY, *her sister, fifteen*
SALLY, *their cousin, twenties*
PHIL, SALLY's *husband, twenties*
GRANDMA *(Marjorie)*, FRANNY, DOLLY & SALLY's
  grandmother
OLDER FRANNY *(She also plays* GRANDMA*)*

An apartment, Sullivan Street, Greenwich Village, 1957

"I believe I essentially remain what I've almost always been—a narrator, but one with extremely pressing personal needs."
—J D Salinger from *Seymour: An Introduction*

for Tim Sanford

(Lights up on a tenement apartment, Sullivan Street, Greenwich Village. 1957. Living room and kitchen are combined: chairs, kitchen table, refrigerator, counter, sofa, etc. Doors to two small bedrooms, one closed, one open. A door to the hallway. [The bathroom is in the hallway and shared.])

(An open window through which we hear the sounds of Sullivan Street—traffic, voices, and those of Bleecker around the corner—distant jazz from a club. [Mostly horns, something like Miles Davis' Sketches of Spain*] Except for what comes from the window, the only light comes from the open bedroom and it is very dim.)*

(Late night. Late June. It is hot.)

(Slowly we begin to hear noises from the closed bedroom, a groan, a cry. A couple are making love. They reach a climax and the woman shouts out.)

(Pause)

(Bedroom door opens, a young man, PHIL, *comes out. He is naked. In the bedroom, a young woman,* SALLY, *sits on the edge of the bed, also naked. They are in their twenties and married.)*

*(*PHIL, *wiping the sweat off his face [then onto some furniture as he passes] heads for the refrigerator. He opens the door—light—and takes out a bottle of beer. He opens it and drinks as he looks out the window; the jazz in the distance.)*

(He breathes heavily, catching his breath; he goes and turns on an electric fan. SALLY comes into the room. As PHIL is turning on the fan)

PHIL: *(Holding up his beer)* You want a—? *(Sip)*

SALLY: Sh-sh. Sh-sh.

(And she gestures toward the other bedroom. They listen for an instant, then relax, smile, even a little giggle as if they have gotten away with something. She nods, and goes to light a cigarette. He hands her the bottle, she takes a big sip, and they both end up looking out the window. He sits with her on the sofa and holds her, kisses her neck, she responds. Sips again, smokes. They listen to the music. She moves to it a bit.)

SALLY: *(After a deep sigh)* God is it hot. There's no air out there. *(Looks at the fan)* Does that reach—? I can't feel anything.

PHIL: Let me try.

(As he stands, a metal object—a baby's rattle—falls on the floor. The noise makes the couple suddenly stop and turn to the open bedroom, expecting to hear something now. There is silence. This at first makes them smile, and SALLY takes another sip or drag, but then she stops, looks concerned at PHIL and heads for this bedroom.)

PHIL: Sh-sh. Don't—.

SALLY: I won't.

(She goes into the bedroom. PHIL plays with the rattle.)

SALLY: *(In the bedroom)* Phil? Phil? *(Louder)* Phil!! Come here!

PHIL: *(Hurrying to the bedroom)* Sally? What's—? *(He turns on the bedroom light—bright light.)*

SALLY: *(At the same time)* Anna? Anna!!!! *(She is nearly screaming now. In the bedroom, she holds up a baby. Screams)* Phil!!!!!!

(SALLY *begins to cry and scream.* PHIL *tries to take Anna from her, but she pushes him away.*)

SALLY: What's wrong with Anna? Something's wrong. Phil!

PHIL: Don't shake her! Anna?

SALLY: Phil, she's blue!

PHIL: Wake up, wake up.

SALLY: Make her wake up! Please, help her, Phil. Help her!

(*He runs out of the bedroom into their bedroom. He comes out trying to put on his pants. The jazz continues from Bleecker Street.*)

PHIL: Oh God, Jesus, Anna, please, please.

SALLY: Sweetie. Wake up, dear. Open your eyes. Mommy's here. Mommy's here. Wake up. Phil!

PHIL: (*Screams*) Sally!!!!

(*Lights fade out*)

Scene One

(*The* OLDER FRANNY *speaks to the audience.*)

OLDER FRANNY: Cousin Sally's and her husband's baby was already dead when they found her in her bed. "Crib death" was what was written on the death certificate. Father said, "Who the hell knows why" would have been just as appropriate.

I was seventeen. This death which swept as a tidal wave over the lives of Sally and Phil, was by the time it reached my distant shore—in Millbrook, New York —but a small almost unnoticed ripple. Perhaps I sent a condolence card. Or maybe I spoke to her briefly during one of her calls with Grandma. Or perhaps it

was merely a "poor Sally" thought I had, which never
even got expressed.

I had, after all, other things on my mind that summer.
There was a boyfriend, with whom I had had my first
sex, and he was now at N Y U. And I loved him.
Though his letters were beginning to get, if not less
frequent, then less—interesting. Was this my fault?
Or his? I was in the midst of my novel about the
rivalries between five sisters in Victorian Yorkshire
England which consumed my summer afternoons.
There was my new stepmother. I thought about her
a lot. My mother I think I was adamantly choosing not
to think about. So that took some time too. And then
there was my name, my new chosen, changed name.
Changed from the matronly and phoney "Frances"
to—Franny. My homage, I liked to call it, to the
beautiful, frail, lost, fair-skinned, funny, faint-prone
heroine of my life and J D Salinger's story. I saw
myself navigating my way through life's sea of phonies.
I was missing only her raccoon coat, but it was still
summer—and my birthday was coming up. Anyway,
as I said, I had a lot to think about.

So when Grandma offered to take my sister and me
on a trip to New York City, it simply didn't occur to me
that our purpose was to console my grieving cousin,
but rather seemed the very understandable fulfillment
of a seventeen-year-old's desire, if not need, to get the
hell out of Millbrook and be hurtled headlong into that
swirl of life called New York.

My little sister, too, had her own plans for this trip.

We took the two-hour train trip from Dover Plains to
Grand Central, and climbed down into the subway and
back up again downtown, up into the noise and music
of the Village. We then walked down Bleecker with its
clubs, doors left open because of the summer's heat,
their sounds like breaths, puffs, exhaled into the street,
into clouds of music we walked through, until we got

here, on Sullivan, in the heart of Greenwich Village,
which for my money and in my dreams was the very
soul and center of the whole goddamn universe.
  So it was on a Tuesday night, in August, 1957,
barely six weeks after the baby, Anna's, tragic and
inexplicable, and by me nearly forgotten death,
that my sister, age fifteen —.

(DOLLY enters from the hallway, small suitcase in hand.)

OLDER FRANNY: And me, age seventeen —.

*(Seventeen-year-old FRANNY enters, looking around
excitedly. She too carries a small bag. PHIL has come in
with them, holding a larger suitcase.)*

OLDER FRANNY: And our Grandma—she was about
the same age then as I am now, so I'll be her—arrived,
ready to spend two exciting and unforgettable days—
of real life.

(OLDER FRANNY will play the GRANDMA throughout.)

*(August. 1957. Eleven P M. Jazz, though much more
percussive than before is now heard through the window,
as well as the sound and noises of the street. SALLY has come
out of her bedroom and is greeting everyone. Everyone is
speaking at once.)*

SALLY: *(To DOLLY)* Look at you. Who let you grow up?!
(Laughs)

FRANNY: Where should we put—? *(Her bag)*

PHIL: Anywhere.

SALLY: *(Over this, continuing to DOLLY)* Does your father
know how much you've grown up?

GRANDMA: He sees her every day.

SALLY: I'm kidding her, Grandma. *(To DOLLY, not letting
go of the subject)* I remember when you used to be—.

PHIL: That's enough, Sally.

SALLY: Enough of what, I don't understand? What am I doing?

(*Awkward moment, then*)

GRANDMA: (*To* SALLY) Oh dear, it's good to see you.

SALLY: (*Pointing to* FRANNY) And you, I knew you'd grow up.

FRANNY: (*To* PHIL) What does that mean?

(*He shrugs.*)

DOLLY: Where's the bathroom?

SALLY: It's in the hall. We share—.

GRANDMA: (*Looking around now*) What a nice apartment. (*It isn't.*) What's that music—?

SALLY: (*Over-excited*) There's a jazz club.

(*To* DOLLY *as if to a child*) You know what a jazz club is?

FRANNY: (*To* GRANDMA) We passed it, Grandma.

DOLLY: (*To* PHIL) The bathroom's in the hall?

SALLY: (*Hearing this*) It's perfectly safe.

FRANNY: I'll go with you.

SALLY: Does she need someone to—?

PHIL: They just got here, Sally. I'll get you a towel—. (*He moves toward their bedroom.*)

SALLY: I put towels on their bed.

(PHIL *heads for the other bedroom.*)

GRANDMA: Are we staying in—? (*There*) How lovely. (*She can barely conceal her disgust for the place.*)

SALLY: You and Dolly will share—. Is that all right with—.

DOLLY: I heard. I've prepared myself.

(Laughter)

SALLY: *(To* FRANNY*)* And you, it's either the couch, or we could put down a few cushions in the bedroom, if that would—.

FRANNY: I'll think about it.

SALLY: *(Onto another subject)* Who's hungry? There's plenty of—.

DOLLY: I have to use the—.

SALLY: *(To* PHIL *who has a towel now)* Phil, show her—.

FRANNY: I'm going with her.

*(*FRANNY *takes the towel and goes out into the hall with* DOLLY. *Awkward moment,* FRANNY *appears again.)*

FRANNY: Which door?

PHIL: The only one on the right.

FRANNY: Do we knock or—?

SALLY: No one's in there. I was just in there.

*(*FRANNY *goes.)*

SALLY: I can't believe how the little one's grown. *(To* GRANDMA*)* Thank you for coming.

(They hug.)

PHIL: Yes, thank you, Marjorie. It's good to see you.

SALLY: *(To say something)* And Fran's a woman now—.

GRANDMA: Franny. We must now call her—Franny. She'll tell you why. *(To* PHIL*)* And how is work?

(He nods.)

GRANDMA: You two are such a lovely couple.

(No one knows what to say, then.)

SALLY: Let me get you something to—.

GRANDMA: We had sandwiches on the train. I brought
sandwiches. We hardly ate them. Are they excited.
(Beat) You won't believe what Dolly's done. You want
to know what she and I are doing tomorrow?

*(*FRANNY *returns with* DOLLY *behind her.)*

FRANNY: *(In the doorway)* I think it's locked.

SALLY: No one was in there a minute ago. Philip,
help them.

FRANNY: I didn't want to push too hard.

PHIL: *(To* DOLLY, *as they go out)* God are you big!

FRANNY: *(Teasing)* What about me?

PHIL: You—you're still a kid and you always will be.

(Tickling her, laughter, the door closes behind them.
Short pause)

SALLY: They're young women. *(Starts to light a cigarette)*
I hope you'll be comfortable. It's not Millbrook.

(A siren goes by outside.)

SALLY: You get used to the....

(She looks around. Clearly GRANDMA *does not know what to*
say. Then pointing to the spare bedroom)

SALLY: That was the baby's room. *(Suddenly changing the*
subject) What has Dolly...?

GRANDMA: *(Confused)* What?

SALLY: You were saying—. Dolly's done some—.

GRANDMA: You won't believe it. You know she's never
been to New York before—.

SALLY: Really? I didn't know.

GRANDMA: You couldn't believe how excited—.
"Peel her off the roof!" That's what her father was
saying this morning. We're seeing *My Fair Lady.*

(SALLY *is confused.*)

GRANDMA: That's what Dolly did. She organized—
all by herself—tickets to.... Her father paid for them
of course—but she wrote off and—. That's what we're
doing tomorrow in the afternoon.

SALLY: That's exciting.

GRANDMA: Aren't you proud of her? I couldn't have
done that at her age. She wrote away and everything.

(PHIL *returns.*)

SALLY: What was—?

PHIL: It was stuck. The toilet door. Franny is staying
with her.

GRANDMA: You remembered to call her Franny now—.

PHIL: She told me.

GRANDMA: Do you know that short story —?

PHIL: I do. (*Beat*) And it's good. Marjorie, don't you
want anything to—? (*Heads toward the kitchen area*)

SALLY: I offered. They've eaten sandwiches. No one is
hungry.

PHIL: What about something to drink? You must be—

SALLY: She doesn't want anything. I asked.

GRANDMA: Actually, I am a little—[thirsty].

PHIL: (*To* SALLY) Why didn't you offer—.

SALLY: I did!

PHIL: You want a beer? There's Cokes, I'll bet the girls
would like—.

SALLY: I'll get them.

PHIL: (*Over this*) I'll get them!

(Pause as PHIL *goes to refrigerator and starts taking out Cokes.)*

PHIL: *(The same safe subject)* Dolly's gotten big, hasn't she?

SALLY: Like she all of a sudden sprang up.
(To GRANDMA*)* You probably don't notice it as—.

PHIL: She notices it. *(Takes out glasses for the drinks)*

SALLY: Maybe they don't want glasses. Kids like to drink from the bottle.

PHIL: We'll give them the choice then.

(Short pause)

GRANDMA: Dolly didn't take a sheep to the Dutchess County Fair this summer. So I suppose that's over.

PHIL: She's growing up.

SALLY: I used to take my sheep. I used to sleep with my sheep overnight. A lot of kids did. *(Beat)* It was great.

PHIL: I'll bet.

SALLY: Bull. You hate the country. You hate animals. You hate—.

PHIL: I don't hate animals.

SALLY: You think all farmers are—.

PHIL: I do not.

SALLY: *(To* GRANDMA*)* He thinks our whole family are—.

PHIL: I do not! *(Beat. To* GRANDMA*)* I don't.

SALLY: *(Changing the subject)* Dolly's never been to New York before. She and Grandma are seeing *My Fair Lady*.

PHIL: *(To* SALLY*)* You wanted to see that.

SALLY: I'm jealous.

PHIL: *(Moving toward the spare bedroom)* Franny says she wants to sleep in there. I'll set up the cushions—.

SALLY: I'll do that.

PHIL: I don't mind.

SALLY: Which sheets are you going to—?

PHIL: Which sheets do you want me to use?

SALLY: *(Exasperated)* I'll do it.

PHIL: I can make up a bed on a floor. I'm not that incompetent.

(They look at each other.)

SALLY: Go ahead then.

GRANDMA: I can help if....

(They ignore her. PHIL goes into the bedroom. We see him through the open door as he makes up the bed. SALLY goes to the refrigerator and starts taking a few things out.)

SALLY: I made a few things....

GRANDMA: Sally, it's after eleven. The kids should be going to bed. *(Pause)* What did you make? *(Goes and looks over the dishes, turns to listen to music)* Does that go on all night? The music.

SALLY: What music? *(Laughs a little too hard)* That's a joke Phil and I.... Yeah. It does.

(FRANNY and DOLLY return.)

DOLLY: What a neat bathroom. I can't wait to take a bath in that tub.

GRANDMA: Phil's making up your bed—

SALLY: So—*My Fair Lady*. Aren't you lucky. I'm jealous. *(Continues to set out food as she talks. To DOLLY)* I have a friend who auditioned for a replacement in that show. She was in my acting class with me.

DOLLY: Really?

FRANNY: *(Looking around)* This is so neat. Look at this.

(She goes to the window. DOLLY *follows.)*

SALLY: Don't get too close to that—.

FRANNY: I'm not going to—.

SALLY: I've told Phil a thousand times we need a bar, an iron bar, so no one.... No child...

FRANNY: I'm not a child.

SALLY: I didn't mean—. Doesn't anyone want something to eat?! *(This comes out almost as a cry, and we see that she is nearly in tears, trying not to cry.)* I made things to eat.

*(*PHIL *is in the doorway.)*

PHIL: *(Impatient)* Sally.

SALLY: *(Crying)* I'm trying not to!

*(*FRANNY *and* DOLLY *are confused, they look to* GRANDMA *who begins to push them toward their bedroom.)*

GRANDMA: You girls have a big day tomorrow—.

DOLLY: Why is Sally—?

PHIL: *(As they approach him, heading for their bedroom, to* FRANNY*)* So college! *(To the others)* Franny says she's looking at colleges!

GRANDMA: *(To* SALLY*)* I didn't tell you, she's going to take a tour—.

PHIL: *(Teasing)* N Y U!

SALLY: *(To* FRANNY*)* I didn't know. No one tells me—.

FRANNY: I have a friend who goes there. And—she wants me to look—.

PHIL: And your father? Doesn't he know? He'd have
a fit if you left Upstate—. *(They are in the bedroom now.)*
I can just hear him: "We have excellent colleges up here,
young lady."

DOLLY: Sounds like Father.

FRANNY: Except for the "Young Lady" stuff. I've gotten
him to stop that. I told him another "Young Lady, Dad,
and this Young Lady is going to burn down one of your
best barns." I meant it too.

*(PHIL, who obviously enjoys playing with these girls, goes
"Ohhh that scared him". GRANDMA goes and hugs SALLY.)*

SALLY: I promised myself I wouldn't do that.

(Another hug, then)

GRANDMA: Your father wants you home. Both of you.
He's got his eye on a nice house. I've seen it. *(Beat)*
Get away from here. And come home.

SALLY: *(Wiping her tears)* I'm an actress, Grandma.
I've got a new teacher. I know he'll take me. He's going
to help me with my singing. That's what I need.

(PHIL comes out of the bedroom.)

PHIL: Is it all right if Franny borrows a robe? She forgot
hers.

*(SALLY nods. PHIL goes back into the bedroom. SALLY gets a
robe from their bedroom, returns.)*

SALLY: *(To GRANDMA)* He won't touch me, Grandma.
He doesn't want me, since...

*(She tries not to cry. GRANDMA takes her hand, she pulls it
away.)*

SALLY: He hates me. And I hate him.

*(GRANDMA watches as PHIL comes out of the bedroom to get
the robe. SALLY crosses and awkwardly hands him the robe.*

He goes into the other bedroom, and suddenly FRANNY
and DOLLY *attack him—they were hiding behind the door.
Screams, laughter, etc, from this bedroom and the over-
excited young women. The night sounds/music and lights
begin to fade.* GRANDMA *shouts: "Now get to bed. Phil,
you're winding them up.")*

Scene Two

*(The middle of the night. The apartment is quiet, except for
soft music coming from the radio in* PHIL *and* SALLY's
*bedroom. No lights are on. No music from the club on
Bleecker Street, it is too late. A little noise from the street)*

*(*FRANNY *comes out of the bedroom, now in one of* SALLY's
*robes. She is trying to make her way to the sink, though is
having trouble seeing; she kicks the leg of a chair as she passes
along the table.)*

*(At the sink, she turns on the tap, and drinks. She notices the
music coming from the bedroom. She slowly heads to the
window where she looks out, lost in thought. A fire truck
passes in the distance, voices from the street.* FRANNY
watches.)

Scene Three

*(Late the next morning. Light streams in from the window.
The noise from the street is alive and present—people,
crowds walking by, sirens, horns, etc.)*

*(*GRANDMA *is cleaning up after breakfast, still in her
nightgown and* DOLLY, *dressed, but a bit dishevelled—
she hasn't combed her hair yet, tucked in her blouse, etc,
stand at the window.* SALLY, *in a robe, sits at the table.)*

DOLLY: *(Looking out)* It's so interesting.

GRANDMA: *(To* DOLLY*)* It's not as much fun as it looks out there.

DOLLY: I didn't say it was fun. I said it was really really really interesting.

SALLY: It's that, Grandma. You can't argue with that.

GRANDMA: Look at that. Look at what he's wearing. Oh my God.

DOLLY: It's summer—.

GRANDMA: *(Going back to cleaning up, half to herself)* On a public street.

(Pause. A church bell chimes in the distance.)

DOLLY: She's still in there?

GRANDMA: *(Picks up the coffee pot)* Should I throw it out—?

*(*SALLY *nods, then.)*

SALLY: No, I'll take it. I could go and knock....

(Door to the hallway opens. FRANNY *enters, dressed, combed, lost in her thoughts.)*

SALLY: Here she is.

(The others just look at FRANNY.*)*

FRANNY: What??? What's wrong? *(Starts to fix her hair)* Why are you looking at me?

SALLY: Nothing.

DOLLY: Phil had to shave in the kitchen sink.

FRANNY: What???? Why did he do that?

GRANDMA: He shaved in the—?

DOLLY: You were still in the bedroom, Grandma. *(To* FRANNY*)* He had to get to work. He works.

SALLY: Dolly—.

FRANNY: What does that have to do with me?

DOLLY: You've been hogging the bathroom, Franny. How long was she in the—?

FRANNY: Why didn't he knock?

DOLLY: *Everyone's* been waiting to use the bathroom—.

FRANNY: Why didn't anyone knock—?

GRANDMA: There's just the one bathroom—and it's not just for us, but for the whole floor. Isn't that right? It's not like home, Franny.

FRANNY: But why—?

SALLY: It's fine. Leave her alone. Philip didn't mind. *(To* GRANDMA*)* It'll give him something to talk about.

FRANNY: There's nothing for him to talk about! Jesus. What did I do? I don't understand.

DOLLY: She always hogs the bathroom. She doesn't think about anyone else needing to use the—

FRANNY: *(To* DOLLY*)* Shut up.

GRANDMA: Girls—.

DOLLY: I've been in there with her. She'll stare at herself in the mirror for—.

FRANNY: Leave me alone! *(Looks at her sister)* What are you talking about? Do you know what you're talking about? Maybe if you took a bath a little more often, you wouldn't have to slap so much deodorant on.

GRANDMA: Franny—.

FRANNY: You think no one can smell it? It's true. Smell her. Go ahead. *(To* SALLY*)* You don't have to sleep in the same room as—.

GRANDMA: *(To* DOLLY*)* I didn't smell—.

FRANNY: You can't smell anything, Grandma.

(Short pause. DOLLY *turns back and looks out the window.)*

FRANNY: Bathroom's free.

(She turns to go into the bedroom. DOLLY *laughs under her breath,* FRANNY *turns back.)*

FRANNY: Why don't you jump?

GRANDMA: Maybe I should get dressed.

FRANNY: *(To* DOLLY*)* Or maybe you need a push—.

(She hurries to DOLLY, SALLY *grabs* FRANNY.*)*

SALLY: Stop it! Stop.

FRANNY: *(Same time)* I wasn't going to—.

SALLY: How old are you two anyway?!

*(*DOLLY *suddenly musses up* FRANNY's *hair and runs for cover.)*

FRANNY: Damn you!

SALLY: Don't swear—.

FRANNY: *(Over this)* What are you—? I just fixed....
(Tries to fix her hair) I'll kill you.

GRANDMA: Who wants to use the bathroom next?

DOLLY: *(Still all of her focus on* FRANNY*)* Sorry to mess up your hair for your big—"appointment."

FRANNY: You shut up, Dolly.

GRANDMA: *(Suddenly)* What big appointment?

*(*FRANNY *doesn't know what to say.)*

FRANNY: *(Under her breath to* DOLLY*)* You are in big trouble.

DOLLY: Me? Really?

GRANDMA: I thought you were just going to walk around the campus with your friend. Do you have an appointment at the college?

FRANNY: No, Grandma. I don't know what my little sister is talking about. But that is usually the case, isn't it? We must all be used to that by now. I should go. Betty's probably waiting for me.

DOLLY: "Betty"???

FRANNY: *(To* SALLY*)* Betty's a friend from home. She goes to N Y U. She promised to show me around. *(Trying hard)* Of course Father says there's a million good schools upstate or in New England, why in the world would a girl want to live in New York City when... When there's all that there, I suppose. *(Looks at* SALLY*)* Betty's two years older. Very responsible. I'll be fine, don't worry. Is my hair—?

DOLLY: Oh God don't let her go back into the bathroom!!

FRANNY: *(Suddenly turns on* DOLLY*)* And—Dolly what are your "big" plans for today?

(This stops DOLLY, *she looks at her sister, then.)*

DOLLY: We're seeing the play. She *(*SALLY*)* knows that.

SALLY: I'm so proud of you for sending off and getting tickets all by yourself.

FRANNY: She's not five years old, Sally. Far from it. *(Starts for the bedroom, then stops)* Oh, you're just "seeing the play." I see. Careful, sister. Now you leave me alone. *(She goes into their bedroom.)*

SALLY: *(Suddenly standing)* We should all get dressed.

DOLLY: *(At the same time)* Grandma we should go—.

GRANDMA: Mind if I use the...bathroom.

SALLY: *(To* DOLLY*)* You've got loads of time.
A matinee's not until two thirty—.

DOLLY: We're going to Gimbels first.

GRANDMA: She wants to go to Gimbels.

DOLLY: Get ready Grandma.

GRANDMA: There's something there she's been looking
for. At Gimbels. She won't tell me what it is. It's a big
secret.

(Smiles, even winks at DOLLY, *and picking up a pile of
clothes she is going to wear, heads into the hallway to the
bathroom. Pause.* DOLLY *goes back to looking out the
window.* SALLY *looks at* DOLLY. *Then, to say something)*

SALLY: So—you like shows too.

*(*DOLLY *nods.)*

SALLY: I love them.

*(*DOLLY *smiles.)*

SALLY: How's your father? Surviving okay?

DOLLY: Sure.

*(*SALLY *doesn't know whether to say more, then.)*

SALLY: I really like your father. A shame about what
you mother did to him—.

DOLLY: *(Interrupting, she doesn't want to talk about it.)*
He's just fine. Really.

SALLY: My Dad thinks the world of him. Of his "little
brother." Funny to think about it that way, isn't it?
His little... Dad says your father's going through a lot,
but who'd know? That's what he says. *(Beat)* You
should have seen the letter your father wrote me after
our baby.... After what happened—.

*(*DOLLY *suddenly turns from the window.)*

DOLLY: Oh my God, Sally, I'm so sorry, I haven't said how sorry I am for what—.

SALLY: I wasn't asking for—.

DOLLY: (*Same time*) No, I know, but—.

SALLY: I didn't mean to—. I know your feelings. You don't have to... It's probably better that you haven't said anything. Let it all—heal.

(DOLLY *is still kicking herself for not saying anything.*)

SALLY: You don't want to just keep—picking at it. Then it'll never get better. So... Don't worry, I wasn't expecting...

DOLLY: I am sorry—.

SALLY: And you guys are just kids.

FRANNY: (*Entering, all dressed, shoes, etc., carrying her purse*) Who's a kid? Don't include me in—.

DOLLY: (*As soon as she sees* FRANNY) Sally was just talking about her baby.

(*It hits* FRANNY *too.*)

FRANNY: Oh God. Sally, I'm so sorry—.

DOLLY: (*Over this*) She doesn't want—. She isn't asking—.

FRANNY: I wrote you, didn't I? I was planning to write you and Phil a long letter—. I didn't know if I should say anything—.

DOLLY: (*Over some of this*) She wants us *not* to talk about it.

FRANNY: That's what I would have thought—.

DOLLY: So it'll heal, she says.

FRANNY: That's why I didn't—.

DOLLY: Right, Sal?

(SALLY *looks at them and nods.*)

SALLY: Whatever you think is best. I don't know.

(*She smiles at her younger cousins, then*)

SALLY: So—Grandma's looking good, I think.
Don't you?

FRANNY: We see her all the time, so—. I'm glad you
think so.

DOLLY: (*Laughing*) Father's finally got her off her little
tractor.

SALLY: She wasn't still—?

FRANNY: Just for the lawn.

SALLY: Still.

DOLLY: Yeah.

SALLY: I'm sure that wasn't easy.

FRANNY: What?

SALLY: Getting Grandma off the tractor.

FRANNY: No. It wasn't.

(*No one knows what to say.*)

SALLY: (*Nods to the bedroom*) I'm sorry if it's a bit messy
in there.

FRANNY: No, it's—.

DOLLY: No.

SALLY: The—cradle, we've been trying to—give away,
but.... (*Looks at herself*) I'm the only one *not* getting
dressed. I better.... (*Moves toward her bedroom*)

FRANNY: I should go. I'm meeting—Betty in—.

SALLY: (*Suddenly*) Not yet! Stay another minute.
I want to show you both something! (*She has run
off into her bedroom. Off*) It won't take long.

DOLLY: What's she...?

(FRANNY *shrugs.*)

FRANNY: I have to go.

DOLLY: Any message you want passed along?

(FRANNY *ignores her.*)

DOLLY: Just thought I had to ask. She'll want to know.

FRANNY: *If* she shows up, Dolly. Have you thought about that? If Mother *deigns* to turn up.

(SALLY *returns with her guitar, tuning it.*)

SALLY: (*As she tunes*) I'm supposed to play for this—. There's a class. He's a fantastic singing teacher. I think he'll take me. But I have to sing.... (*Tunes, then to* DOLLY) I told you one of my friends auditioned for—the show you're seeing. *My Fair Lady.* And I've got a better voice than she does. (*Strums, to a worried* FRANNY) If you have to go.

FRANNY: No, I'm.... I have time. How long do you—?

SALLY: You really want to hear it? Both of you? Really?

(*"Sure", "Yeah", etc from the girls*)

SALLY: I didn't know what to choose, then I thought a kind of jazzy—. (*Starts to strum cords and begins to play and sing a slightly jazzy version of* Hernando's Hideaway *from* Pajama Game. *Sings*)
I know a dark secluded place
A place where no one knows your face
A glass of wine a fast embrace
It's called Hernando's Hideaway
Olé

(*Girls listen politely, without criticism.* SALLY *smiles, strums louder as she gets more and more into it, even making castanet sounds on the face of her guitar with her fingernails.*)

SALLY: *(Sings)* All you see are silhouettes
And all you hear are castanets
And no one cares how late it gets
Not at Hernando's Hideaway.
At the Golden Finger Bowl or any place you...

(She stops, feeling self-conscious, even embarrassed. During the song, GRANDMA appears in the doorway, mostly dressed now. When SALLY stops playing)

GRANDMA: That's so good, Sally.

FRANNY: Terrific, Sal. Really. I'm sure that teacher's going to love it.

SALLY: You're just saying—.

FRANNY: No. I mean it. I do. Ask Dolly. I have to go.

DOLLY: It was great.

FRANNY: I'll see you tonight. I'll be back tonight. *(And she hurries out.)*

GRANDMA: Where is she meeting...?

DOLLY: Betty. I don't know. But she knows.

(SALLY has continued to pluck the guitar.)

SALLY: *(To no one)* I love that song. It's so much fun.

(FRANNY bursts back in.)

FRANNY: Sal, the phone's ringing out there.

(We hear it in the hallway.)

FRANNY: What should I...?

SALLY: *(Handing GRANDMA the guitar)* I'll get it.

(She follows FRANNY out into the hallway, leaving the door open.)

DOLLY: We have to go soon, Grandma.

(Phone stops ringing, SALLY has picked it up.)

DOLLY: You should get dressed, come on.

GRANDMA: I'm almost ready. (*Hands* DOLLY *the guitar and heads for the bedroom. Stops*) I only heard the end, but that sounded...good. Did it to you?

DOLLY: It did. Grandma.

GRANDMA: It's nice to hear her sing.

(*She goes into the bedroom. Outside a siren goes by.* SALLY *hurries back in and runs to the window and shouts.*)

SALLY: Franny!!! Franny!!!

GRANDMA: (*From the bedroom*) Is anything—?

SALLY: It's fine, Grandma. (*To* DOLLY) She heard me. I know Franny heard me. She just didn't want to hear me. It was your father.

DOLLY: Father? What's wrong? Is something—?

(SALLY *suddenly sees her with the guitar.*)

SALLY: Don't touch that! Put that down! I just tuned it!

(DOLLY, *stunned, puts the guitar down.*)

SALLY: (*Suddenly guilty*) I didn't mean it that way. I didn't mean you couldn't touch it. I'll teach you to play a few chords, if you want. It's just that when someone doesn't know how to...

DOLLY: Sure. I'm not going to touch it.

SALLY: I didn't mean—!! (*Stops herself. Trying to be calm, then turns back to* DOLLY) Do *you* know where she's meeting this guy? You know about the guy? Of course you do. Is he her boyfriend?

(*No response*)

SALLY: Grandma's going to have a fit. She's my responsibility. If you come and stay with me, I think it's only fair...

DOLLY: How did Father find out about the guy?

(SALLY *looks at her.*)

SALLY: Your stepmother found a letter in Franny's bureau.

DOLLY: What was she doing in Franny's bureau?!

SALLY: *(Over the end of this)* I don't think that makes any difference now!

DOLLY: She shouldn't be in our rooms!

SALLY: He read me part of this letter! How this guy has a friend with an off-campus apartment. How this friend is away this afternoon. How he's got the key, everything but the size of the bed! Your father's so upset. She doesn't know what she's doing. She's a kid.

DOLLY: I hate her. Not my sister.

SALLY: I don't know what to tell... *(Looks toward the bedroom)* Your father's ready to get on a train.

DOLLY: He won't. He just says things like that. Maybe now they'll stay out of our rooms.

SALLY: She's only seventeen. When I was seventeen—.

DOLLY: You going to tell Grandma?

SALLY: Won't your father tell her when you get home?

DOLLY: I don't think anyone tells Grandma too much anymore. *(Short pause)* My stepmother was looking for Franny's diaphragm.

(SALLY *turns, confused, when she hears this.*)

DOLLY: Last week she accused Franny of owning one. Franny denied it of course.

(SALLY *suddenly laughs.*)

SALLY: Where would Franny get a dia—?

DOLLY: But she brought it with her. So that's why she didn't find it.

(GRANDMA *comes out, with a sweater.*)

GRANDMA: Will I need a sweater? Is it going to be like yesterday?

SALLY: It's going to be warm, Grandma.

(GRANDMA *goes back into the bedroom to put back the sweater.*)

SALLY: (*To* DOLLY) So this—"guy". It's nothing special. Something she does all the time. Since she's got the diaphragm...

(DOLLY *shrugs.*)

SALLY: I'm sick. Just don't tell Phil. He's a real prude when it comes to certain things. It's the Midwest in him. And he still thinks of you girls—as kids.

(GRANDMA *comes out, straightening herself.*)

GRANDMA: You've got the tickets?

DOLLY: Yes, Grandma.

GRANDMA: (*Not listening, to* SALLY) Phil gave us four tokens before he left for work this morning.

SALLY: He told me he was going to do that. You sure you don't want to take a—[cab]?

GRANDMA (*To* DOLLY) What is so important about Gimbels? Look at the mess we've left. We shouldn't leave you with—.

SALLY: There is no mess. Please. Go. And have a wonderful time. I hear it's a terrific show.

GRANDMA: (*To* SALLY) You think I look sophisticated enough for a Broadway show?

DOLLY: Good luck with the audition.

SALLY: What???

GRANDMA: *(To* DOLLY*)* I don't want to look like I come from the boondocks.

DOLLY: The singing audition. To get into that—.

SALLY: Oh right. Thanks! Bye!

GRANDMA: *(To* DOLLY*)* You'd tell me if I didn't look right. Your Grandfather wouldn't, he'd let me—.

(Door is closed. They are gone. Silence. Street noise. SALLY *does not know what to do with herself. She fiddles with the guitar, starts to play, stops. She takes the guitar into her bedroom. She returns and begins picking up. Outside the window she hears children playing. She goes into her bedroom and turns on the radio. Music plays. She returns to get her cigarettes. Hears the children and goes to the window to watch. As she sits on the sofa,* OLDER FRANNY *[still of course dressed as* GRANDMA*] enters and speaks to the audience.)*

OLDER FRANNY: I hadn't heard Sally call after me; or if I had it hadn't registered as anything more than one more sound among the millions and millions of sounds which make up Sullivan Street.

*(*SALLY *lies back on the sofa and curls up.)*

OLDER FRANNY: At the corner I waded into Bleecker, as one wades into any fast-moving river, cautiously, but with pleasure, and hurried—if you can be said to hurry when you are watching everything —toward the Riviera Cafe.

*(*SALLY *has fallen asleep.)*

Our meeting spot. My boyfriend had sent me the address. I expected to find him waiting, impatient, with a "why-are-you-always-late" look upon his face. The kind that I could only wash away—with a kiss. But he wasn't there, waiting for me. *(Beat)* I took a table

outside and ordered coffee. I think it was the first time
I ever ordered coffee in a restaurant. I watched the
people go by. The couples. The attractive young men
in their sleeveless summer shirts. I felt like you feel on a
beach with the waves breaking across your ankles, legs,
thighs, and then running away. That's how the people
outside the Riviera came and went. Like waves. I could
sit here all day, I said to myself. *(Beat)* There was a
phone booth on the corner and the first two times I
tried my boyfriend his line was busy. The third time
he picked up. I've been waiting at the Riviera, I said.
Did I get the time wrong? *(Short pause)* You see, he said
in a rather—happy voice, he'd met this girl, just the
weekend before, and he really wished he could tell
me in another way—I deserved that—and by the way,
there's lots of fun things I could do in New York by
myself, did I want a list? And hey, would I like to meet
his new girl, she's real real nice, and the two of us
would really really get along, and to this day I
remember not so much what he said, but the smell in
that phone booth, a mixture of stale cigarette smoke,
some half-eaten thing that had sat in the sun too long,
and urine. Anyway, I hung up on my boyfriend, and
threw up in the booth. Now if a teenage girl throws up
in a phone booth in the middle of Millbrook, half of the
town would be there to find out what was wrong and
to tell your parents. Suffice it to say that in New York or
at least in Greenwich Village people are more respectful
of your privacy. At least that's how I like to think of it.
  I went back to my table and paid for my three coffees.
I felt a little faint and found the bathroom—a tiny, dirty
room with a hook to lock the door. I sat on the toilet
seat, rubbed a wet towel across my face and tried to
stop crying.
  I think I did faint. But I guess didn't hurt myself when
I fell. Someone shouted through the door to see if I was
all right. I suppose they'd heard this thud or something

or maybe just my sobbing.

I left the Riviera intent on spending the rest of my one day in New York walking and seeing first-hand what I'd imagined a million times. But instead, I found myself walking the few blocks back to Sullivan Street, staring for who knows how long at the fire escape on the front of the building which for all the world now looked like an insect climbing up, then walking up the three echoey flights of cold stairs, until I was back here.

(Door opens, FRANNY *comes in, her clothes messy, her eyes red from crying. She stands in the doorway.)*

OLDER FRANNY: Where I'd convinced myself I'd first change my tear- and vomit-stained clothes, but where I also knew, in my heart of hearts, I'd never leave for the rest of the day.

*(*SALLY *does not stir. She is asleep on the couch. At first* FRANNY *hadn't noticed her, but now she does.)*

OLDER FRANNY: I'd expected to find the apartment empty, which is why Sally'd given me my own key.

(She sets the key on the table.)

OLDER FRANNY: But it wasn't. Sally was still there, still in her nightclothes, curled up on the sofa, asleep.

*(*FRANNY *notices the music playing in the other room. She watches* SALLY *for a moment.)*

OLDER FRANNY: What I didn't know then, and wouldn't know for years, was that Sally had had no intention of going out that day. Just as she'd had no intention of going out the day before or the day before that. Just as she'd no intention of ever leaving her apartment again.

(She watches SALLY*.)*

OLDER FRANNY: And this is how she'd spent every day, since the death of her baby. *(Beat)* At the time though,

I knew none of this. At the time, I thought only about
how much I hurt. And how much I needed a bed to cry
on.

(FRANNY *goes into the bedroom, closing the door.*)

Scene Four

(*Middle of the afternoon*)

(*The radio is still on in the bedroom, though a different song
is heard. The street noise has a different quality—slower,
easier than in the morning. Hallway door opens, PHIL enters
carrying a couple bags of groceries. [He does all the shopping,
chores, etc. since SALLY no longer leaves the apartment.]*)

(SALLY *is still asleep, curled up on the sofa. She stirs when he
closes the door, but does not wake up.*)

(PHIL *takes the bags to the kitchen table and begins to
unpack.*)

(*Throughout the entire scene the music plays on the radio in
the bedroom.*)

SALLY: (*Waking up*) What's...? (*Sees* PHIL) What time is it?

PHIL: (*Putting groceries away*) About four in the
afternoon.

SALLY: Anyone...? (*Else here*)

(PHIL *shakes his head, then*)

PHIL: I see you haven't even gotten dressed.

(*Short pause*)

SALLY: (*Smiling*) Come here. Come here. Sit with me.

(*He ignores her.*)

PHIL: (*Unpacking*) I got some nice chops for tonight.
He trimmed the fat off for me. I'm getting good at this.
Look at these.

(Holds one up. She looks at the chop.)

PHIL: *(Finally)* Have you even washed? Your grandmother's here. Your cousins. What are you doing?!

SALLY: *(Suddenly smiling, changing the subject)* You want to hear something about my little cousin—?

(He turns away.)

SALLY: I was going to my audition!

PHIL: No you weren't.

SALLY: I was!! Don't you talk to me like that, you creep! *(Beat)* I was going.

(He unpacks. She smokes.)

SALLY: I don't sleep at night. I fell asleep. I must look a mess. *(She looks at him.)* You could say something. "No honey, you don't look a mess. You look sweet." "I love it when you just wake up." "I love that little girl look you have then, I—." I remember, Phil. Word for word. *(Looks at him)* He's even stopped listening. *(Big sigh, then)* What was I—? My little cousin, Franny.

You know what she's doing right now? Little Franny's out fucking some boyfriend. That's what all this was about. Her wanting to come down here. See a college? Lies. *(Explaining)* The stepmother up there, what's her name?—found a letter. What the hell she was doing going through her stuff, I don't know, but...

Right now, in some crappy student apartment, she's fucking him. Maybe even next door. *(Pretends to listen)* Sh-sh. *(Laughs)*

(The door to FRANNY's bedroom has slowly opened at little. Neither PHIL nor SALLY notice this.)

PHIL: Let her fuck, so what? What's wrong with that?

SALLY: *(Suddenly)* What's wrong with fucking? I don't know, Phil. You tell me. *(Looks at him. She gets up and*

*looks at him across the kitchen table. As she leans, she nearly
exposes her breasts.)* What is wrong with it? *(She tries to
touch him, but it is clear he can't even touch her.)* What else
besides the chops are we having for dinner?

PHIL: Mashed potatoes. String beans. I thought we'd
go get Italian ices for dessert. The kids I thought would
like that—.

SALLY: What kids? Have you heard a word I said?
I wouldn't call running off with—. And she's got tits
like—. Bigger than mine. I suppose you like that.
And she knows what she's got too. *(Beat)* So do you
think she's attractive?

PHIL: Sally, what are you talking about?

SALLY: Is she the type you'd fuck?

(No response)

SALLY: You've got to be fucking someone, and it
certainly isn't me.

PHIL: Don't be pathetic.

SALLY: A little late for that.

(He tries to ignore her.)

SALLY: I should get dressed. After all, we have guests.
(Beat) I was dreaming of our baby. That's the dream
you woke me from. *(Trying to make a joke)* You should
apologize for that. *(Then)* That's why I woke up smiling.
She was all right, you'd be happy to know. She was
maybe three. She was running. And smiling. She could
talk. I loved her little voice. When Dolly was three I
used to babysit her, so maybe that's why.... The spark.
(Beat) Anna running through the park. Or maybe it was
in the country. Grandma says Dad would help us get
the house. Back home. I told her—I'm going to be an
actress. I am an actress! I need to live here. I need all the
city has to—.

PHIL: So get out of the house.

(This stops her, then she tries to stay calm.)

SALLY: I will. *(Heads to the bedroom. Stops in the doorway)*
I'd expect you to be a little more—understanding.
We all have our crutches... *(Beat)* Look at you, Phil.
Sometimes I think we need to look at you. You used
to say going to church was for your parents and other
hypocrites and phonies. Remember saying that?

PHIL: You've done this already, Sally.

SALLY: *(Continuing)* That you didn't need that crap.
Real *thinking* people saw through all—.

PHIL: I went once! I shouldn't have told you.

SALLY: But you did. *(Forces a smile)* And now who's
the hypocrite, Phil? Who's the phoney just like your
parents? Who got on his little knees and prayed:
Oh dear God, help me! Help me! Take away these
evil thoughts I have about doing harm to myself!

PHIL: *(Erupts)* I shouldn't have told you!!

(Short pause)

SALLY: That—was a reaction. Thank you.

*(She goes into the bedroom. PHIL takes out a beer and opens
it. In the bedroom, SALLY takes off her nightgown and puts
on a skirt. She comes back out, straightening the skirt.
She is naked from the waist up. She comes up to PHIL,
pretending to fix her skirt.)*

PHIL: Don't walk around like that in front of the
window.

SALLY: Why? It's our home. *(Walks in front of the
window)* Actually, I seem to recall *you* saying something
like that—to me. *(Half to herself)* "Sal , it's our home.
We can walk around any way we want." *(To him)*
I think this was right after your suggesting I take off

all my clothes. *(Teasing, trying to be seductive)* "You mean, I don't have to wear...?" And you put your finger to my lips, and whispered: "You're home. You don't have to wear anything." *(Beat)* "You don't have to wear that." And you touched me. "Or that." "That." *(Looks at him, smiling)* Remember? And we didn't close the shades either. *(She goes up to him.)* And *I* said "You don't have to wear—."

PHIL: Get dressed, Sally. You want your grandmother to come home and find you like this?

SALLY: You mean, like I am? Like we are?

(He turns away. SALLY approaches him from behind. She presses up against his back. She rubs her breasts against him, trying desperately to interest him. She reaches around to try and hold him. He is shaking his head. Gently he pushes her hands away. She reaches down and tries to touch his groin, he pushes her harder away. And she erupts. Suddenly she starts hitting him on the head and back, while at the same time trying to press her breasts against him, as if two contradictory impulses were happening to her—her anger and her need. Neither say anything or make a sound. SALLY just continues to hit—PHIL makes little effort to protect himself—and press herself on him, touch him, get him to touch her: a grotesque moment of self-abasement. The door to FRANNY's bedroom suddenly closes. PHIL and SALLY stop when they hear the noise. PHIL goes to the door and knocks. Nothing. As he reaches for the knob, the door opens—FRANNY is there.)

SALLY: *(Suddenly seeing FRANNY)* What are you doing here?!! *(Turns to PHIL)* Did you know she was—? *(She covers her chest.)*

PHIL: No.

FRANNY: I was—writing in my journal... *(She holds up her journal that she has been clutching.)*

SALLY: How long have you been here?

FRANNY: I just got in.

(They stare at her.)

FRANNY: I was writing. In my journal. I just started.
Excuse me.

Scene Five

*(In the dark, a voice [*GRANDMA'S*] calls out.)*

GRANDMA: Franny! Dinner!

*(*FRANNY *opens the bedroom door:* GRANDMA, SALLY,
PHIL *and* DOLLY *are finishing setting the small kitchen table
for dinner. They are talking as they finish setting things out
and taking their seats at the crowded table. Street noise from
the window. Early evening)*

GRANDMA: *(To* SALLY*)* Your father's even picked out
one house.

SALLY: Which one? Do I know it?

(A glance at PHIL*)*

GRANDMA: On Chestnut. The white one with the gables?

SALLY: What happened to the couple who—?

GRANDMA: He's retired. And the stairs are too much.

SALLY: *(To* PHIL*)* Remember that house? I drove you by
it—.

GRANDMA: *(At the same time)* And they have a son in
Baltimore, so they're thinking—.

SALLY: How did Father know it'd—?

GRANDMA: Did you ever talk to him about it?

SALLY: *(To* PHIL*)* I didn't. I swear. Anyway, we're
staying here.

(FRANNY *has slowly moved to the table.*)

FRANNY: Where am I supposed to—.

SALLY: Get a chair and push in. This isn't formal.
(Laughs to herself. To FRANNY*)* You didn't hear us
setting the table?

FRANNY: I—.

*(Everyone is digging in, passing the food, commenting:
"Dig in." "Looks great." "These chops are so lean."
"Phil had them cut off the fat. He's a good shopper." etc.
While* FRANNY *drags a chair to the table and sits, squeezing
in. Out of this innocuous table conversation comes)*

SALLY: Phil was saying when we were making
dinner—. Tell them. *(Reaches over and touches his hand)*

PHIL: About?

SALLY: *(Smiles to everyone)* Work today. Your guest.

GRANDMA: What??

PHIL: An important writer came to the office today.
It's a publishing office so how strange is that?
(Laughs. No one else does.)

GRANDMA: Who was this writer?

PHIL: I don't think you'd—.

SALLY: Tell them.

PHIL: Edmund Wilson. Do you know...? *(No one does.)*
He's...fat. *(Laughs)* Mr Farrar and Mr Cudahy were
showing him around. We had to almost stand at
attention. The three of us in publicity. He won't give
interviews. He won't promote his books at all. He even
showed us a little card he hands out that says "I won't
give interviews. I don't give autographs. I don't—
whatever." He seemed to think that was clever. *(Beat)*
And I suppose maybe it is—to anyone except the
someone whose job it is to promote his damn books.

(Takes a bite of food) He's a good writer though.
Worth the trouble. That's what I'm told.

(Pause. They eat. No one is interested in PHIL's *story,
but he continues.)*

PHIL: He'd sold his new book to another publishing
house—Doubleday. So they were trying to woo him
back. That's what it was all about. I learned this....
(Short pause) Anyone want to know any more about it?

(No response)

GRANDMA: *(Turns to* FRANNY*)* How was your tour of
the college?

SALLY: Yes, let's hear about that.

GRANDMA: Did you like it?

FRANNY: Sure.

GRANDMA: You met up with your friend all right?

*(*SALLY *looks at* FRANNY.*)*

FRANNY: I did.

GRANDMA: She was helpful?

FRANNY: She was.

SALLY: *(Being mean)* Tell us what you liked most about
the college.

*(*FRANNY *looks at the others, then)*

FRANNY: The library's neat. I liked that.

SALLY: You liked the library. Spend much time in the
library with your friend?

FRANNY: Enough. But she had a lot of studying to do,
so that's why—as you both know—I came back early.
(Takes a bite) So how was *My Fair Lady*? I haven't heard
a—.

GRANDMA: We've talked about that. Dolly will tell you later—.

SALLY: Tell her now. She should know just what a little conniving sister—.

PHIL: Stop it.

SALLY: *(To* FRANNY*)* Your sister planned, it appears, a little more than a trip to a show. They're in Gimbels, she and Grandma and....

(Turns to GRANDMA *who says nothing)*

SALLY: They're looking at sweaters? It was sweaters, right?

GRANDMA: Yes.

SALLY: And suddenly Dolly looks at her watch. Oh my God, she says, let's go to the perfume counter. Why? says Grandma. You want to look at sweaters, don't you? But Dolly nearly drags Grandma to the perfume counter. The clock strikes twelve and guess who is waiting there?

FRANNY: Mom.

(Reaction from the others)

SALLY: She knew. She's a part of this. *(To* GRANDMA*)* I told you this.

FRANNY: *(Over this, to* DOLLY*)* Was she alone or did she—.

DOLLY: Alone.

SALLY: She wouldn't have the guts to bring him. Isn't it enough to—. And what's Grandma supposed to do?

GRANDMA: She was made up like a—.

DOLLY: She looked beautiful.

FRANNY: I'm sure she did. How long were you with her at the perfume counter, Dolly?

GRANDMA: A couple of minutes.

FRANNY: Oh.

SALLY: Then they had lunch.

FRANNY: *(Amazed)* Together? I didn't know you were going to have—.

DOLLY: Mom bought us lunch.

FRANNY: *(To* GRANDMA*)* Yours too, Grandma?

*(*GRANDMA *shrugs as if to say "What could she do?"* FRANNY *starts laughing.)*

SALLY: What's funny?

PHIL: *(To join in)* Where'd you eat?

DOLLY: *(Looking at* FRANNY*)* Some place called—Dempseys??

SALLY: *(Over this to* FRANNY*)* And she went to the show too. Little miss arranger had worked everything out.

(This gets FRANNY *laughing again.)*

SALLY: She'd sent away—.

FRANNY: Who paid for—?

DOLLY: Dad.

(A burst of laughter from FRANNY*)*

DOLLY: But Mom's paying him back.

SALLY: He won't take money from her.

DOLLY: *(To her sister)* We had seats together. Mom sat next to me. She misses us so much, Franny.

*(*FRANNY *stops her laughing.)*

SALLY: *(After a quick glance at* PHIL, *to* FRANNY *and*
DOLLY*)* What that woman did to your father. You
don't treat a husband like that.

PHIL: She fell in love.

GRANDMA: I think it's best if we don't say a word about
this to their father.

(Short pause. FRANNY *stands, taking her plate to the
counter.)*

PHIL: You're done? You haven't eaten—.

FRANNY: I'm not hungry.

(She looks to DOLLY.*)*

SALLY: *(Eating)* Your first time in New York. And you
arrange tickets, lunch, a meeting with—. We're going
to have to watch her, Franny. She's sneaky.

SALLY: *(To* PHIL*)* Think of the position she put Grandma
in. What could she be thinking?

PHIL: *(Eating)* That she wants to see her mother.
That's all she's—.

SALLY: That woman's a whore.

*(*DOLLY *gets up and takes her plate to the counter, joining
her sister.)*

SALLY: *(To* GRANDMA*)* And I'm serious you're really
going to have to keep an eye on Dolly. If this is how—.
Lying to us. Stealing—.

PHIL: What did she —[steal]?

SALLY: Money for the theater tickets, from her father.

DOLLY: *(To* SALLY*)* Mom's paying that back.

SALLY: *(Continuing)* Money for a trip that was supposed
to be about—something else. I know we're not that
much older than those two, Grandma, but that only

means we [Phil and her] remember what it's like.
At their age. So there are problems, but you have to
control yourself. That's what growing up means, girls.
(Back to GRANDMA*)* Aren't I right? *(*GRANDMA *hesitates,
then nods.)* This is for your benefit, girls, please. I'm not
trying to be mean. *(To* PHIL*)* Am I?

PHIL: No.

*(*SALLY *reaches over and touches* PHIL*'s hand. He eats.
To* GRANDMA*)*

PHIL: I remember sitting with their *(*FRANNY *and*
DOLLY*'s)* father—he took me into his study—.
After their mother had left. I felt sort of flattered that
he chose me, though maybe he was talking to anyone.
(Laughs) But I was flattered. And all he talked about
was how much he loved those two girls.

*(*GRANDMA *nods.)*

PHIL: How they're his life. His two daughters.

SALLY: *(To* PHIL*)* I don't think he talked to everyone.
I think he chose you. Just like *my* father chooses to
confide in you. *(To* GRANDMA, *explaining)* When we
visit? You raised two great sons, Grandma. How did
you do it?

GRANDMA: Luck, I suppose—. *(Laughs to herself)*

SALLY: What?! *(Looks to* PHIL, *then back to* GRANDMA*)*
Tell us what's funny.

GRANDMA: Those two boys always weren't so good.

SALLY: *(A little too excited)* My father?!! Oh!!

(Laughs, then suddenly turns to FRANNY *and* DOLLY *at the
counter)*

SALLY: Listen to this, girls. Grandma's going to tell us
about our fathers—when they were boys.

*(*FRANNY *and* DOLLY *don't move.)*

GRANDMA: They were—wild boys.

(Big whooping laugh and clap of the hands from SALLY. *Smile from* PHIL*)*

GRANDMA: Now they're—the two most straight-laced men you'd find—. Anywhere.

*(*FRANNY *and* DOLLY *certainly agree with this.)*

GRANDMA: But—.

SALLY: Didn't they fight a lot as boys?

(Clearly SALLY *has heard these stories before.)*

GRANDMA: Fight? They were at each other's throats.

(Laughter from SALLY*)*

GRANDMA: I remember—.

SALLY: *(Excited to* PHIL*)* Here comes a Grandma story. *(Touches* PHIL*'s hand again)*

GRANDMA: *(To* PHIL *and* SALLY, *sincerely)* You are such a wonderful couple. *(Quickly continuing)* When Edward won that red bicycle in the grocery store contest. Robert was beside himself.

*(*SALLY *looks back to the girls on "Robert". Clearly Robert is the girls' father.)*

GRANDMA: "Thou shalt not covet thy brother's bike." Isn't that one of the ten commandments?

(Laughter. GRANDMA *obviously isn't that funny, but she's getting a great response from* SALLY. *Lights begin to fade.* FRANNY *and* DOLLY *remain at a distance, stone-faced.)*

GRANDMA: Anyway—he "borrowed" it—. And there he is riding his brother's bike, coming down a gravel hill, and he tries to turn—. I can still see Edward's face. I've never seen something *that* red....

(The last image we see is that of FRANNY *and* DOLLY
watching from a distance.)

Scene Six

(Later that night)

*(Jazz music is heard coming from the window. It will play
throughout the scene. The room is mostly dark, only a single
light is on.* FRANNY *and* DOLLY *are alone together.* DOLLY
is holding a letter. FRANNY *sips a beer.)*

DOLLY: She's so beautiful. I guess I forgot that. After
two years you forget. When I was nearly at the perfume
counter—.

FRANNY: Dragging Grandma.

DOLLY: *(Smiles)* Yeah. And she came around—.

FRANNY: *(Trying not to sound interested)* What was she
wearing?

DOLLY: Dark blue dress, with a white print. With
straps, little cape. The dress went right below the knee.
A funny wonderful little hat, she wore angled. Mom
can wear things that other people.... Gloves.

FRANNY: White?

(Beat. DOLLY *shakes her head.)*

FRANNY: Dark blue?

*(*DOLLY *nods.)*

DOLLY: You going to open it? *(The letter)*

*(*FRANNY *ignores her.)*

DOLLY: She didn't seem—.

FRANNY: *(Interrupting)* What?

DOLLY: I mean after what we'd been told —. She seemed to—. She started crying, Franny. *She* started....

FRANNY: Mom cries easily.

DOLLY: Does she?

(Beat)

FRANNY: Yeah. It means nothing.

DOLLY: I thought Grandma was going to have a heart attack.

(FRANNY *smiles.*)

DOLLY: I think it took her a half an hour before she realized that I'd.... You know—.

FRANNY: That you hadn't just run into—.

DOLLY: Yeah.

(They both laugh, then silence.)

DOLLY: Open it. It's to you.

(FRANNY *hesitates, then takes the letter and opens it. Finds a photo, looks, then has to close her eyes—the emotion is too great.)*

DOLLY: How old are you there?

FRANNY: *(Suddenly)* You know I don't believe a word she says. And you shouldn't either. She's only going to hurt you. If she had wanted to see us—.

DOLLY: She said she's tried. She's had a lawyer try. She's even called Father and begged—.

FRANNY: I can't imagine Mother begging for anything. Certainly not for us. *(Starts to put the picture and the unread letter back in the envelope)* This was a mistake Dolly—.

DOLLY: She asked why we didn't answer any of *her* letters.

FRANNY: What letters?

DOLLY: She's written tons of letters—to both of us, she said.

FRANNY: And you believe her?! Oh Dolly!

(Short pause)

DOLLY: *(Picking up the Playbill of* My Fair Lady*)* I can't even remember the show. As soon as the lights went down, I guess so Grandma couldn't see or do anything to stop us, Mom reached over and took my hand and held it in hers.

(Hands FRANNY *the Playbill.* FRANNY *looks through it.)*

DOLLY: Then she pulled it to her, and pressed it against her chest. Then she kissed it. I put my head against her shoulder. She stroked my head. She touched my cheek. I looked up at her. We cried through the whole play. *(Beat)* At the intermission, Mom went outside to smoke a cigarette. Grandma tried to buy me some candy, but I just followed Mom. Grandma said something about how "you haven't given up that awful habit, have you Jennifer?" The cigarettes.

*(*FRANNY *nods. She understands.)*

DOLLY: Grandma wanted me to go inside with her, but I wouldn't. Then Mom snapped open her purse— I remember the purse—with thin gold stripes and a gold band—.

FRANNY: I don't remember the purses. *(Tries to laugh)*

DOLLY: And took out a photo. And said here, Dolly, this is "my man." *(Short pause)* That's what she said, called him—"my man." Grandma made this awful sound and sort of ran away—for an instant, 'cause she was back in a second, but not before I had a chance to look... Back inside, she slipped it into my hand, and I hid it in my program.

(FRANNY *realizing, shoves the Playbill back at her.* DOLLY *opens it and takes out the photo of their mother's lover.*)

DOLLY: Here he is.

FRANNY: I don't want to see—.

DOLLY: Look, Franny.

FRANNY: (*Erupts*) I don't want to see—"her man"! Get it away from me!

(*She pushes the photo away. Hallway door opens and* SALLY *enters, having used the bathroom.*)

SALLY: I'm done. Thank God I sneaked in there before Franny, or—. (*Smiles*) But I learned my lesson there.

(FRANNY *ignores her. So she smiles to* DOLLY, *as if it was* DOLLY *she'd been speaking to.*)

DOLLY: (*To say something*) Think what I go through at home.

SALLY: You must have the patience of a saint.

DOLLY: Thank you. I think I do.

(SALLY *moves toward her bedroom.*)

FRANNY: (*To* SALLY) Can I go down to that—. (*Jazz*)

SALLY: No. The night's over for you, young lady. And for all of us as soon as Grandma and Phil get back from their walk. It's.... (*Starts to look for the time, then*) And besides, I'd have thought after your day, you'd be very very tired. (*Forces a smile. Then half to herself as she heads for the bedroom*) When I was seventeen, I didn't even know what a diaphragm was!

(SALLY *has gone into her bedroom.*)

DOLLY: She knows about—. Father called—.

FRANNY: I heard.

DOLLY: *(Over this)* They'd found a letter, about how you were going to meet—.

FRANNY: So what? Does Grandma know—?

DOLLY: I don't think she told her—.

FRANNY: I don't care what they think. They're idiots. They are complete phonies. *(Beat)* And so is Mom.

DOLLY: That's not true.

FRANNY: How did she know about my dia—? *(Seeing* DOLLY'*s guilty face)* Forget it. *(To herself, mumbling)* Father and his bitch. *(Suddenly, hits the chair or sofa)* Shit!

(Beat)

DOLLY: And Mom is not a phoney.

FRANNY: Believe what you want.

DOLLY: And by the way—she did say that she'd seen me in the play.

FRANNY: What??

DOLLY: The play I was in. She saw it.

FRANNY: No she didn't. She didn't even know about you being in the—.

DOLLY: I'd told her about it. I'd called her and—.

FRANNY: You called her? Mom? When? You didn't have her number—.

DOLLY: I had gotten it out of Dad's desk. There's a— divorce file. You know Father, he's so— (Organized). I knew it was there. And I found it and I called her and I told her because I thought she'd really really want to know that I got the part of the young girl in *Our Hearts Were Young and Gay.* I thought she'd really want to know about my costume. Because she always made our costumes with us for Halloween. So...

(FRANNY *just watches her sister, who is close to tears.*)

DOLLY: And she couldn't wait to see me in the play, she said. I didn't ask her, I didn't make her, it's just what she said. *(Beat)* And then she wasn't there.

FRANNY: *(Smiles)* Yeah.

DOLLY: But she *did* come. And she asked me if I liked her flowers. I never got any flowers. Did I?

FRANNY: I don't remember any. What do you mean Mom was there?

DOLLY: Remember the little boy playing the steward on the ship? And how he came on stage all proud and was suppose to be saying: "All ashore who's going ashore!" but instead shouted: "All aboard who's going ashore." And then cried? *(Beat)* Mom said that was her favorite part. I hadn't said anything about it, she told me.... Her favorite—except of course for me. *(Smiles. Short pause)* How could she have known—?

FRANNY: Father probably told—.

DOLLY: They don't talk!

FRANNY: You believe her?

(DOLLY *nods.*)

FRANNY: That she was there?

DOLLY: In the back, so Father—

FRANNY: So no one could see—. *(Stops herself)* You never got any flowers. They were probably never sent—.

DOLLY: When we left today—and we were hugging. Again I thought Grandma was going to die, but.... We're hugging and she says how much she loves me. And you. And then she said...

(FRANNY *waits and listens.*)

DOLLY: —her last words today were—. She said: "don't trust your father".

(Pause. The jazz plays in the distance.)

DOLLY: How was *your* afternoon?

FRANNY: Great. We pretty much wore out my diaphragm.

DOLLY: Is that what happens? They wear out?

(SALLY enters in a robe, and goes to the couch to read a magazine. She turns on a lamp, then suddenly realizes.)

SALLY: Oh I know what you two have been doing.

FRANNY: What?

SALLY: You little snoops.

DOLLY: What are you talking about?

SALLY: You've had the lights out.

(They look at her, confused.)

SALLY: So you can spy on... *(Nods toward the window)*

FRANNY: At what?

SALLY: Aren't they there? *(Looks out the window)* Across the street. One floor higher. They often "forget" to close their shades. *(Looks at the girls. A statement)* You haven't seen them. So what have you been looking at?

DOLLY: We haven't been looking at—.

FRANNY: *(Same time)* What is she talking about?

SALLY: A couple. About Phil's and my age. They walk around—without—anything. Right past the window. One, then the other. Sometimes one'll run past, then he'll hurry behind her. Then you don't see them for a while. *(Looking)* I figure off to the left—that's their bedroom. They have a bathroom, I think. And to get to that they must have to pass... *(Beat, looking out)* That's

the—study or whatever. They've got a T V. You see the
blue light sometimes. I've seen him sit—there's a chair.
When he sits you can see his arm. Sometimes I think
she sits with him or—on him. All you see is his arm,
and her, like— *(Gestures)*. You sort of imagine what
they're doing. *(Beat)* Maybe they're just watching T V.
Maybe they're talking politics. *(Smiles)* But that's not
what it looks like—with the arms. Once his arm was
like— *(Back to us)*, and hers—turned the other way
(Facing us), and it's—lower, so she's, and at a certain
moment, they held hands... *(Beat)* You two probably
don't understand, but you will when—.

FRANNY: You're imagining that she's sucking him off.

(Short pause)

SALLY: That's correct. *(Looks at* FRANNY*)* Don't think
you can shock me. You can shock your grandmother.
You can shock your father, but I see right through you.
I see who you are—*and* who you think you are. And
there's a real big discrepancy, my dear. *(Pause. Looks out
the window. Smiles to herself)* Sometimes, I think they
look at us. We often—forget to close the curtain. And
we walk around—Philip and me, like... I don't know
when I've last worn pajamas or a nightgown. And
Philip of course wears nothing. *(To* FRANNY*)* I'm sorry
if this—.

FRANNY: If this what??!!

SALLY: I mean—you two are just kids. *(Smiles. Notices
the beer on the floor next to* FRANNY*)* Is that a beer you
have? Did Philip give you that?

FRANNY: I took it myself.

*(*SALLY *nods, thinking.)*

SALLY: I remember when I was your age, sneaking my
first drink—.

FRANNY: It's not my first—.

SALLY: *(Over this, to* DOLLY*)* Swallowing it really fast
I thought I was so neat. So grown-up. I wasn't going
to listen to what anyone said, I felt I could do what I
wanted. Then the room started spinning, and then there
was my father holding my head over the toilet bowl as
I barfed up my guts. *(Laughs)* It's not easy growing up.
I know. Believe me, Franny, I know all about it. I've
been there. *(There is nothing to say. Finally she looks
toward the door.)* How long are Grandma and Phil
going to be out?

(No response)

SALLY: I think I'll read in our bedroom. *(Picks up her
magazine)* Goodnight, Dolly. *(Looks to* FRANNY, *but
decides not to get too close)* Goodnight Fran. I
mean—"Franny." That's so cute. *(Goes into her bedroom)*

FRANNY: What a cow.

DOLLY: She's okay. She's gone through a lot.

*(*FRANNY *picks up her beer and takes a sip.)*

FRANNY: Want some?

*(*DOLLY *nods. She takes a sip.)*

FRANNY: Want your own?

*(*DOLLY *nods.* FRANNY *goes to the refrigerator, takes out
another beer, opens it, hands it to* DOLLY *and lights a
cigarette, as)*

FRANNY: I hate her guts.

DOLLY: *(Picking up* FRANNY's *letter)* You going to read
this?

*(*FRANNY *ignores her, then looks out the window.)*

FRANNY: Someone's turned on the lights over there.

DOLLY: You know she (SALLY) told Grandma and me this incredible dream she had. This morning when you were in the bathroom. She told us about what she dreamed last night?

(FRANNY *just nods and continues to watch out the window, sipping her beer and smoking. Jazz plays off.*)

DOLLY: She dreamed she'd just moved into a new town. Her family had moved—. She was a kid, and they had a dog which they brought with them? And as soon as they moved in the dog died. (*Beat*) And her father— I think he says something like, let's not take it to the vet, that's just a waste of money. So she's given the job to bury the dog. But then a neighbor, a new neighbor, because they just moved in and didn't know anybody yet, says that if she buries it, it'll only smell up the place, so he says she should cremate it. "What's cremate?" she asks.

FRANNY: She didn't know what—?

DOLLY: In her dream. She's that young.

(FRANNY *nods.*)

DOLLY: "Burn it," he tells her. So she pours gasoline over the dog and lights a match. (*Beat*) And as the dog goes up in flame—it starts to howl and scream something awful. She even mimicked what it sounded like. (*Tries to demonstrate*) I can't do it like she did.

(FRANNY *now turns to* DOLLY *and is interested or fascinated.*)

DOLLY: So she runs inside and gets her dad's twenty-two, hurries out and chases around this dog that's on fire and shoots it. Well all the neighbors are out now and watching, and everyone is horrified at what this girl's done—set a dog on fire and then shot it. And she knows that as long as she lives in this new town, that's what people will think of her. That's how she'll forever be known. *(Beat)* That's it. That was her dream. Amazing? You know the essay I have to write this summer about "a real interesting character"? Well... *(Gestures toward* SALLY*)* It's going to write itself.

FRANNY: I think she's pathetic.

DOLLY: She lost her baby, Franny.

FRANNY: *(Shrugs, then)* So get over it.

(The hallway door opens, and GRANDMA *and* PHIL *return from their walk. She is very tired, he holds her by the elbow.* FRANNY *and* DOLLY *hide the drinks and cigarette.)*

PHIL: Sit down. I'll get you a glass of water.

FRANNY: What's—? *(Wrong with Grandma)*

GRANDMA: I'm fine.

DOLLY: Sit down, Grandma.

FRANNY: Sit down.

PHIL: Your Grandma's a little tired. It was a bit longer walk than she thought. And it's been a long day.

GRANDMA: I'm just sleepy. Really. What time is it?

PHIL: Nearly eleven.

GRANDMA: I never stay up this late. Where's—?

FRANNY: She's gone to bed.

PHIL: Her light's still on—.

GRANDMA: Don't bother her. *(Yawns)* I should just go to—. *(Taking the glass of water)* Thank you.

(Sips. Tries to catch her breath. Others watch this and say nothing. Feeling she is being watched)

GRANDMA: I'm not used to stairs.

SALLY: *(Off)* Grandma! Is that you?

PHIL: We're back!

GRANDMA: I should go and say goodnight to that beautiful wife of yours. *(Goes into the bedroom)*

PHIL: *(To* DOLLY*)* You should be getting to bed too, shouldn't you?

DOLLY: I'm not tired.

PHIL: What's that? *(He has noticed the beer.)* Have you been—?

DOLLY: Maybe I will go to bed. Goodnight. Night. Goodnight, Franny. *(Kisses her)* Phil.

(As he bends to kiss her, she tickles him and runs away.)

PHIL: *(To* FRANNY*)* What about you?

*(*FRANNY *shakes her head.)*

PHIL: Never going to bed?

*(*FRANNY *smiles and shrugs as* GRANDMA *comes out of the bedroom.)*

GRANDMA: Remind me to buy her a nice nightgown for Christmas. I'll use the bathroom if that's—.

(But before she can head there, DOLLY *runs out of their bedroom, carrying her nightgown and hurries into the hallway to use the bathroom.)*

PHIL: *(As* DOLLY *runs off)* Let your Grandma—.

GRANDMA: Maybe I'll get ready for bed first. I'll say my goodnights in a minute. *(Tries to smile and heads off)*

FRANNY: She looks exhausted.

PHIL: She was fine. Then all of a sudden about four or five blocks away, I thought she was going to fall down. We had to stop every few feet. That's why we're...

FRANNY: Dolly put her through a lot today. *(Beat)* I think she thought she'd never see my mother again. And of course she has to be polite. Even—or maybe especially—when she hates someone she has to be polite. That must be hard. *(Beat)* Not that I would know.

(PHIL is picking up the room.)

PHIL: I don't think a fifteen year-old should be drinking beers. *(Noticing the ashtray)* And smoking cigarettes.

(Beat)

FRANNY: Who cares what you think?

(He turns toward his bedroom.)

PHIL: *(Noticing)* She's turned off her light.

FRANNY: Better go to bed then.

(He continues to pick up. She listens to the jazz.)

FRANNY: You want to take me to that club?

PHIL: No.

FRANNY: I'm old enough.

PHIL: I know.

FRANNY: Then why not? *(Takes her beer back from him. Sips)*

PHIL: *(Incredulous)* What are you doing?

FRANNY: I didn't finish that. I want to go there.

(He looks at her, sipping her beer, a flirty pout on her face, and he approaches her, and suddenly dives at her and tickles her. She tickles back. DOLLY enters from the hallway, now in her nightgown, sees what is happening and runs to join in: "Get him! Get him! Not me, him!" "Stop! Stop!" Then as PHIL is pushed off the sofa onto the floor)

PHIL: I give up! I give up!

SALLY: *(Off)* Phil? Philip?

(Pause. They stop and listen.)

SALLY: Phil?

(He gets up and goes into their bedroom. Muffled voices from the bedroom: "What are you doing out there?" "Nothing." "Aren't you coming to bed?" "In a few minutes.")

DOLLY: *(To FRANNY)* Don't forget the letter.

(PHIL comes out of the bedroom, stopping at the doorway.)

PHIL: *(To SALLY in the bedroom)* Would you like the door closed?

(We don't hear the answer, but PHIL doesn't close the door. As he turns back to the girls)

PHIL: *(To DOLLY, pointing)* You—to bed.

DOLLY: Night. What about—?

FRANNY: I'm coming. Let Grandma use the bathroom first.

PHIL: Goodnight.

(DOLLY goes off to their bedroom. Pause. Jazz plays.)

FRANNY: So you don't wear anything to sleep in?

PHIL: What??

(He looks at her. She smiles. Then she turns and looks out the window.)

FRANNY: They just turned their lights off.

PHIL: What are you talking about?

(She stares at him.)

PHIL: *(Finally)* What hasn't my wife told you about?

(DOLLY comes back out.)

DOLLY: Grandma's asleep. She hasn't used the bathroom. Should I wake—?

PHIL: Let her sleep.

FRANNY: Is she still in her clothes—?

DOLLY: No, she changed.

FRANNY: Good.

(DOLLY starts to go back, stops.)

DOLLY: Franny, you can use the—.

FRANNY: Thanks. I know. Goodnight.

(DOLLY goes into the bedroom. PHIL sips from FRANNY's beer.)

PHIL: "Franny". I think that's really neat, by the way. I've been meaning to say that.

FRANNY: What?

PHIL: Changing your name. Because of the Salinger story. I think it's an incredible story.

FRANNY: Me too.

PHIL: Obviously or you wouldn't have—.

FRANNY: Do you think she's pregnant or having a nervous breakdown? In the story. *(Beat)* Franny.

PHIL: I know. I—maybe it's both.

FRANNY: That's good. I hadn't thought of that.

PHIL: That's—what a lot of people think now. Anyway, it's a neat thing to do. If only my name were Zachary, then I could—

BOTH: —be called Zooey!

(They laugh. Short pause. PHIL looks toward his bedroom, then)

PHIL: You've read "Zooey"?

FRANNY: In the town library. The school library doesn't get *The New Yorker*—.

PHIL: I wouldn't think—.

FRANNY: And Dad forgot to get it in Poughkeepsie, when he went....

PHIL: I have a copy. But it's the only one—.

FRANNY: No, no I —

PHIL: And it sold out in like—. *(Snaps his fingers)*

FRANNY: I heard. Though not in Poughkeepsie.

(He smiles. An awkward pause)

PHIL: *(Finally)* Lying in your bathtub, smoking cigarettes, talking to your mother, who's sitting there, smoking cigarettes. And she's a vaudevillian. To me— that's New York. That became New York. You try and think, so what is the difference between Ann Arbor and New York? I think of Zooey in the bathtub. I don't know why really. *(Smiles at her)* It seems so—I don't know. Sometimes this place can seem so scary. New York.

(FRANNY nods.)

PHIL: And sometimes it's like it just sort of wraps its arms around you. The sounds, people...*(Drifts off in thought, then)* You think you'll come here to go to school?

(FRANNY shrugs.)

PHIL: What does your boyfriend say?

FRANNY: He's—begging me to come.

PHIL: I'm sure.

(Another pause. The jazz plays. FRANNY plays with the letter.)

PHIL: *(Noticing the letter)* What's—?

FRANNY: From my mother. I haven't read it yet. *(Short pause)* What do you think he's going to write next? Salinger.

(PHIL *shrugs.*)

FRANNY: Could be a million things. There's so much we don't know about—the twins. Waker? In the conscientious objectors' camp? What's that about? I think what Salinger's got to do is start putting things together. Show how the Glass family fits together. Right now it's just—bits, fragments—.

PHIL: Fantastic bits—.

FRANNY: True. But I think he's only begun something.... Something that is going to define our time.

PHIL: Huh.

FRANNY: I can't wait.

PHIL: Me too. *(Beat)* I'm going to bed when I finish this.

FRANNY: Don't drink too fast.

PHIL: I won't.

FRANNY: Sip and you'll remain standing. Father's advice.

(PHIL *sighs, wipes the sweat off his forehead.*

FRANNY: Earlier this summer I was in a show at home. I was a flapper. In the chorus. In my high school gym. Something to keep the kids out of trouble. *(Smiles)* God was it hot in that gym. My dress stuck to my backside. *(Looks down at her backside)* Kept having to pull it off. In the middle of a dance. *(Not thinking about what she is saying)* I don't know if I want to be in theater or not. Dolly wants to, but...I like books. I think I'm pretty enough though.

PHIL: You are.

FRANNY: How's Sally doing with her acting? She doesn't seem to be doing much work right...now.... *(Realizes this is the wrong thing to bring up)* I should go to bed. Goodnight.

(She stands. Looks at PHIL, *then leans over and kisses him on the cheek. As she does, he turns to her. And they kiss on the mouth. She sits next to him, and they look at each other. She touches his face. He looks her over. He suddenly gets up and closes his bedroom door and turns off the lamp. He comes up behind her, touches her on the shoulder. She looks up at him, and as she watches him she reaches under her skirt and takes off her underpants. She puts her head against his hand. He kisses the top of her head. She suddenly turns and they kiss passionately. She rubs her hand across his chest and unhooks his pants belt. Still kissing, she unzips his fly. Her hand is in his crotch, his hands are up her skirt, under her blouse. When at the height of this heavy petting,* PHIL *suddenly breaks away.)*

PHIL: No. I can't. Franny, this isn't right. This is wrong.

(He tries to get a hold of himself, breathes deeply. She watches him. He zips up his pants, hands her her underpants. She watches. He then takes her hand and squeezes it, and goes into his bedroom, closing the door. FRANNY *cries. She tries to get ahold of herself. She turns on the lamp, notices the letter from her mother. This makes her sob. She hides the letter under magazines and continues to cry.)*

(Lights fade. Music fades.)

(Immediately lights come up and new, wilder jazz music plays from the club on Bleecker. It is two hours later.)

*(*FRANNY *is still on the sofa. She is awake and listening. She is crying, and can't sit still, can't settle.)*

(From PHIL *and* SALLY's *bedroom: the sounds of the couple making love. As they approach climax, the noises/sounds/ cries become more and more violent, animal-like, and profound, as if something deep, painful, uncontrollable is being touched and released.* FRANNY *listens, then stands and goes into her bedroom and closes the door.)*

Scene Seven

(The next morning. Street noise is heard out of the window.
DOLLY *is packing in the bedroom.)*

(In PHIL *and* SALLY's *bedroom doorway:* SALLY *is finishing
up* Hernando's Hideway, *on the guitar for* PHIL *and*
GRANDMA *who is at the sink cleaning up.* PHIL *is getting
dressed.* SALLY *is still in a robe.)*

SALLY: *(Singing)*
At the Golden Finger Bowl or any place you go,
You'll meet your Uncle Max and everyone you know.
But when you go to the spot that I am thinking of
You will be free
To gaze at me
And talk of love!

*(*FRANNY *enters from the hallway and goes into her bedroom
to finish packing.)*

SALLY: *(Singing)*
Just knock three times and whisper low
That you and I were sent by Joe

*(*DOLLY *enters with her suitcase.)*

SALLY: *(Singing)* Then strike a match and you will know
You're in Hernando's Hideway, Ole!

(Appreciative reaction from PHIL *and* GRANDMA*)*

SALLY: He's a fantastic teacher. I think he'll take me.

GRANDMA: Of course he will... *(Etc)*

SALLY: *(To* PHIL*)* What do you think?

PHIL: I think you're good. I always have. He'd be a fool
not to take you.

GRANDMA: I can't believe she hasn't played that for you, Phil.

(FRANNY *comes out with her suitcase.*)

SALLY: I didn't think he wanted to hear it.

GRANDMA: Of course he did. Phil loves to hear you sing. Did you hear what he said? What time is it?

SALLY: Oh God, the time!

PHIL: We're fine. There's—.

SALLY: What time's their train?

GRANDMA: I better strip the bed.

(GRANDMA *heads for her bedroom.*)

SALLY: You don't have to do that. Phil?

PHIL: (*Following* GRANDMA) I'll do that, Marjorie.

(PHIL *sees* FRANNY.)

FRANNY: We're packed.

GRANDMA: (*As she enters the other bedroom*) I love Sally's singing, don't you, Phil?

(GRANDMA *goes into the other bedroom to strip the bed.*)

SALLY: (*To the girls*) Everyone slept so late. We slept so late. (*Smiles to herself*) There's no time for breakfast. I'm sorry—.

FRANNY: Oh we're not hungry. Are we, Dolly?

(DOLLY *is hungry, but says nothing.*)

FRANNY: She's fine.

SALLY: There's some bread from last night—.

DOLLY: I don't want to miss the train. Dad's meeting the train.

SALLY: *(Smiles at them, then)* I wish you could stay longer. I really do. It's been really good having you here. And next time, *(To* FRANNY*)* we'll have that boyfriend of yours over for dinner too.

*(*PHIL *brings out* GRANDMA*'s suitcases.)*

SALLY: Phil was saying how he'd like to meet him.

*(*PHIL *hurries back into the bedroom.)*

SALLY: Grandma should tell you two about the house she went to see last night with Phil. He was telling me about it.

FRANNY: What house?

SALLY: It's just a few blocks away. Where she lived.

FRANNY: Where who lived?

SALLY: Our Grandma.

PHIL: *(Off)* Sal, Majorie's making the bed!

SALLY: *(Heading for the bedroom)* Grandma, I told you I'd make it!

DOLLY: In Greenwich Village? Grandma lived in Greenwich Village?

FRANNY: When was this?

*(*SALLY *has disappeared into the bedroom. Voices are heard off.)*

DOLLY: I don't understand.

FRANNY: Me too. I don't understand anything.

*(*SALLY *suddenly appears in the bedroom doorway.)*

SALLY: *(Back to* GRANDMA*)* You think I should? Phil? Maybe I will. Maybe I'll come. *(Heads for her bedroom)* Is there time? I have to get dressed.

GRANDMA: *(Coming out of the bedroom. To the girls)* Sally's coming with us to the train station.

PHIL: *(To* GRANDMA*)* She's coming with us. She's
getting dressed.

FRANNY: When did you live in Greenwich Village,
Grandma?

GRANDMA: A million years ago.

FRANNY: You lived in New York City??

GRANDMA: I must have told you that. I don't want to
be one of those old ladies who is always repeating
themselves.

PHIL: They don't know. Tell them. They're interested.

SALLY: *(Coming out of the bedroom, getting dressed)*
There's probably a lot you don't know about your
grandma. Did you go inside? I meant to ask you that.

PHIL: I wanted to ring the bell.

GRANDMA: *(To the girls)* I remember leaning out the
second-floor window of that house and watching the
soldiers march down Fifth Avenue, on their way to war.

FRANNY: What war??

GRANDMA: Us girls waving our scarves. *(Winks at the
confused* DOLLY*)* Accidentally letting one go. Float down
past the boys, to see if they would look up. And they
did. *(Laughs)*

*(*SALLY*, listening, laughs maybe a little too hard from the
other room. She is keyed-up.)*

GRANDMA: People were screaming. My father, your
grandfather was one of them. He says he probably
marched right past me. But I never picked him out.
There were so many boys.

DOLLY: How long did you live in New York City,
Grandma?

GRANDMA: A whole year. Maybe a little more.
While Grandpa was at war.

PHIL: *(To* FRANNY*)* The First World War.

GRANDMA: It's all changed now. It's all different.

(Short pause. Everyone is a little confused, then, explaining)

GRANDMA: The house. Where I used to live. I told you
why I was sent to the city?

PHIL: You told me, Marjorie.

GRANDMA: It's incredible now that you think about it.

SALLY: *(Off)* I haven't heard this.

GRANDMA: *(Continuing)* But at the start of the war, your
great grandfather had to hire all these day workers for
the farm. All these—men. There was a lot of pressure
to grow things for the war effort. So he needed a lot
of men? Whatever kind of men he could get. *(Smiles)*
But he worried that maybe it wouldn't be right for
me...So he sent me here! Sent me to New York.

(The girls look at her, incredulous.)

FRANNY: He sent you to New York City to be safe from
men????

*(*GRANDMA *nods.)*

FRANNY: Incredible.

(They burst out laughing.)

GRANDMA: *(Over the laughter)* And it took my father
a whole year to figure out what he'd done! And did
I have fun!

(More laughter. Then SALLY, *now dressed to go out, comes
out.* PHIL *and* GRANDMA *are nearly overcome with emotion.)*

SALLY: I'm ready, we should go.

GRANDMA: We have everything? We haven't forgotten anything?

FRANNY: I don't know.

GRANDMA: Let me just check... (*Heads back into the bedroom*)

SALLY: (*Following her*) If you did, we can always mail it—.

(PHIL *is handing a magazine to* FRANNY.)

FRANNY: What's this?

DOLLY: What is it?

PHIL: An old copy of *The New Yorker*. With a wonderful story in it.

FRANNY: I can't take this. It's your only copy—.

DOLLY: Let me see—

FRANNY: No, you'll rip it.

(*She takes it.*)

SALLY: (*Coming back out with* GRANDMA) What's that?

PHIL: Nothing.

FRANNY: The Salinger story—

DOLLY: (*To* PHIL) Why are you giving *her* presents?

FRANNY: Because he likes me better!

DOLLY: He does, does he?

(DOLLY *grabs* PHIL *and tickles him, he fights back, tickling.*)

SALLY: (*To anyone who will listen*) I can't believe I'm taking you to the train!

GRANDMA: Come on, girls. We're going to be late. Leave Phil alone. Come. Pick up your bags.

(SALLY *suddenly joins in the tickling.*)

GRANDMA: We have to go. Phil, why don't you walk with your wife.

(They continue to tickle as she pushes them out.)

GRANDMA: Let's go. Girls, let's go. Girls!

(They go out into the hallway, still trying to tickle each other. GRANDMA *stays behind and again becomes the* OLDER FRANNY. *She speaks to us.)*

OLDER FRANNY: And so I went home that summer. And tried to finish my Victorian Yorkshire novel— with no success. And tried to forget a boy—with a good bit more success. And tried to find a much better hiding place for my diaphragm.

Nine months later, my cousin Sally and Phil had a new baby. They came up to show her off, Uncle Edward took them to see the house on Chestnut, and they never left.

I did read Mom's letter—a few billion times. Dolly, my clever little sister, organized an unescorted "shopping trip" that Christmas to New York City. We were to meet Mother in front of Saks. She appeared down Fifth Avenue, through a light snow, amidst the haze of the street lamps, her fur collar framing—that beautiful face. Like a vision—that is how she appeared to me; and that is just about how real, sadly she proved to be. Dolly disagrees, and says I just should have spent time with her—like she did. *(Shrugs)* Grandma lived only another five years. Women, it has recently dawned on me, die young in my family.

And little Annie? The baby? She's buried in Queens. For a while there was talk of moving her to Millbrook. But that stopped years ago. I think she's been forgotten.

(Short pause. Street noise continues from out the window.)

OLDER FRANNY: As we get old, we start to see the— *(Searches for the word, then)* —fragility of—well everything. *(Short pause)* But when we're young, thank God—we are oblivious.

(Suddenly FRANNY *charges back into the room. From down the hall cries of "Franny!" "We're going to miss the train!" "We can send it to you!" etc)*

FRANNY: *(Shouting back)* I'll just be a second!

(She looks around, then hurries to the sofa, desperately searching for something she's forgotten. The OLDER FRANNY *watches. Young* FRANNY *flips over magazines and finds what she is looking for—her mother's letter. She sighs, folds it. Then she suddenly notices something else. Sticking out between the cushions in the couch: her underpants from the night before. She grabs them, looks around, doesn't know what to do. She tries to hide them on her body, then slides them inside the pages of* The New Yorker *she is carrying, smoothing down the pages, as she hurries out shouting.)*

FRANNY: I'm coming!!!

*(*OLDER FRANNY *looks out the window, as the streets sounds continue: they are alive, music in the distance from Washington Square, cars, laughter, church bells, siren, and so forth.)*

END OF PLAY